Fear of the Unknown is the Greatest Fear of All

BY HILARY LAWRENCE

ILLUSTRATED BY KATHERINE SUMMERVILLE

The King of the Jungle roared: "Gather round!
You'll never believe what I just found.
Right behind our Baobab tree,
There's something strange you all must see!

When I was out for my morning stroll,
I narrowly missed a deep, dark hole.
On bending down to look inside,
I couldn't believe my big round eyes.

There was a beast in the hole with a mean-looking stare.
Sitting all alone, watching me from its lair.
Alarmed, I roared – I was ready to attack –
But the creature in the hole just roared right back!"

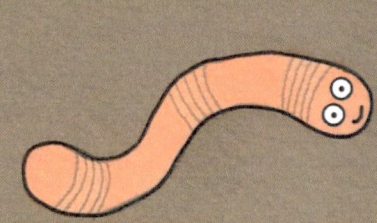
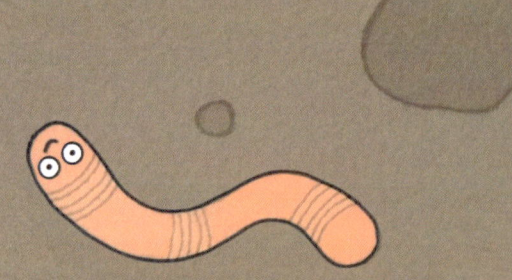

I bellowed, "Show yourself immediately!
How dare you roar and challenge me!
If you ignore me and don't obey,
There will definitely be a price to pay!"

"But the beast in the hole did not come out.
He's waiting till night-time, I have no doubt.
This beast could be our worst nightmare,
Brave as a lion, with a deadly glare.

Maybe he'll eat us one by one?
Or hunt and chase us all just for fun!
For our children's sake, we need to know.
Is this monster a friend or foe?

We can work this out – I know we can.
Luckily, I have a clever plan!
Fox, your hearing and night vision,
Make you my choice to complete this mission!"

"Try to get a good look at his face.
Report back tomorrow. Same time. Same place."

"Fox, tell us, what did you see?
Did you see the monster that roared at me?"

"I did. My plan was to use surprise.
So I crept up at sunset in a clever disguise.

But the beast was disguised, just like me!
How did it know? How could it be?
It just glared at me without looking away.
Cunning as a fox, that's what I'd say!"

"Oh!" said Lion, "Oh me, oh my!
I really am too young to die!
It's brave as a lion, cunning as a fox.
Only one thing for it: your turn, Ox!

Ox, no animal has to be told,
How you are steadfast, strong, and bold.
We're relying on you to crack this case.
Report back tomorrow. Same time. Same place."

"Ox, tell us, what did you see?
Is he a monster? Do you agree?"

"I agree. He's a monster," Ox replied,
"I planned to make him terrified!
I thought if I carried a tree on my back
As a show of strength, he wouldn't attack.

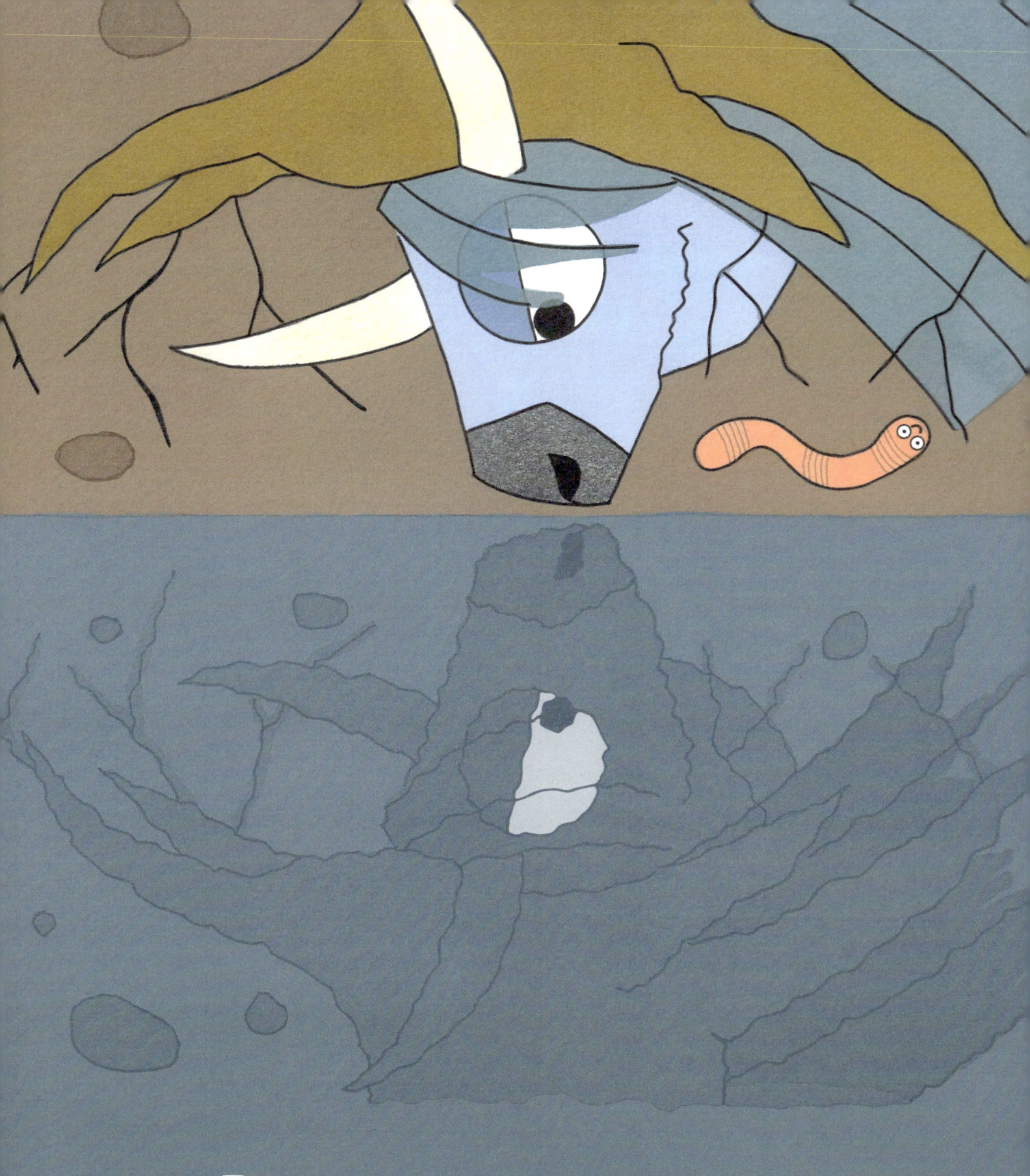

But when I looked in the hole, I could see,
He had the same plan – to intimidate me!"

"Oh dear," said Lion, "Heavens alive!
We must catch this beast if we want to survive.
It's brave as a lion, cunning as a fox.
Now we know it's as strong as an ox.
We'd better beware and take great care.
Only one thing for it: Your turn, bear!

Bear, your claws are the mightiest in the land.
Let's show this beast we have the upper hand.
Try to scare him from his base.
Report back tomorrow: Same time. Same place."

"Bear, please tell us, what did you see?
Did you find his hole by the Baobab tree?"

"I did, I found it," replied the bear,
"Ox's footprints led me there.

"I was holding a big bone in my paw,
And an even larger one in my jaw.
But the beast had the greatest bone I've ever seen,
Clenched in his teeth so fierce and mean."

"Oh, bother!" said the lion, "Mercy me!
We don't want to end up as this beast's tea!

"It's brave as a lion, cunning as a fox.
It's terrifying and **strong as an ox**.
It can **scare a bear** with its terrible growl
Only one thing for it: Your turn, owl!"

Owl, your knowledge is second to none.
I'm convinced you can get this job done!
Use your brain to explain this case.
Report back tomorrow. Same time. Same place."

"Owl, tell us, what did you see?
Please say you've worked this out for me!"

"We have a problem," Owl replied,
"This beast makes me tremble; I'm terrified!

I flew up close despite my fear,
And shouted a threat for him to hear:
"I can outsmart you, I'm the wisest of birds."
But he replied with the very same words!"

"Good grief!" said Lion, "Glory be!
We need to stop him - do we all agree?
It's **brave as a lion, cunning as a fox**,
It can scare a bear, and is as strong as an ox.
Now we know, it's as **wise as an owl**,
And the chances are it's on the prowl!"

"United we stand, divided we fall,
So let's work together, for one and for all!
Prepare to meet him face to face.
We'll leave tomorrow. Same time. Same place."

The animals walked towards the Baobab tree,
Extremely nervous about what they would see.
Lion roared, "On the count of three,
Put your head in the hole, and bellow with me!"

"If you come quietly, we won't attack!"
But the very same words came roaring back.
"Wait," said Owl, "I'm beginning to wonder,
If we might have made an embarrassing blunder?

It sounds like an echo bouncing back,
And now that my eyes get used to the black

I see you, lion, and I see you, fox.
I see you bear, and I see you, ox.
It appears to me, on close inspection,
We've been frightened by our own reflection!

Water in the hole is acting like a mirror.
We have all made such an error!"
The animals laughed till they could laugh no more.
They had never laughed so much before!

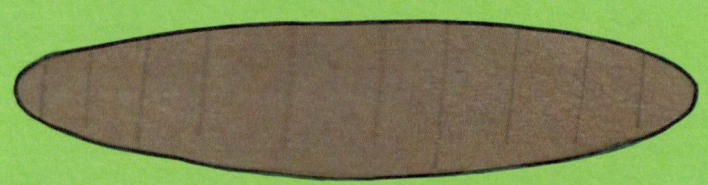

And as tears of relief rolled from Lion's eyes,
He said, "This is such a big surprise!
It is true – for now, it's clear to see:
Things are not always what they seem to be!"

www.ingramcontent.com/pod-product-compliance
Lightning Source LLC
Chambersburg PA
CBRC091203070526
44583CB00008B/187